URBAN LEGENDS • DON'T READ ALONE!

BLOODY MARY

This series features unsolved mysteries, urban legends, and other curious stories. Each creepy, shocking, or befuddling book focuses on what people believe and hear. True or not? That's for you to decide!

45th Parallel Press

Published in the United States of America by Cherry Lake Publishing
Ann Arbor, Michigan
www.cherrylakepublishing.com

Reading Adviser: Marla Conn MS, Ed., Literacy specialist, Read-Ability, Inc.
Book Designer: Felicia Macheske

Photo Credits: © Leszek Czerwonka/Shutterstock.com, cover; © leungchopan/Shutterstock.com, 5; © ARTFULLY PHOTOGRAPHER/Shutterstock.com, 7; © CREATISTA/Shutterstock.com, 8; © percom/Shutterstock.com, 11; © tobkatrina/Shutterstock.com, 12; © Captblack76/Shutterstock.com, 14; © Tom Tom/Shutterstock.com, 17; © Frolova_Elena/Shutterstock.com, 19; © Lario Tus/Shutterstock.com, 20; © alexan888/Shutterstock.com, 23; © Andrew Mayovskyy/Shutterstock.com, 24; © szefei/Shutterstock.com, 27; © Photographee.eu/Shutterstock.com, 29

Graphic Elements Throughout: © iofoto/Shutterstock.com; © COLCU/Shutterstock.com; © spacedrone808/Shutterstock.com; © rf.vector.stock/Shutterstock.com; © donatas1205/Shutterstock.com; © cluckva/Shutterstock.com; © Eky Studio/Shutterstock.com

45th Parallel Press is an imprint of Cherry Lake Publishing.

Library of Congress Cataloging-in-Publication Data has been filed and is available at catalog.loc.gov

Cherry Lake Publishing would like to acknowledge the work of The Partnership for 21st Century Skills.
Please visit www.p21.org for more information.

Printed in the United States of America
Corporate Graphics

TABLE OF CONTENTS

Chapter One

SLUMBER PARTIES GONE WRONG

What's a slumber party? What happened to Katie and her friends? What happened to Sara and her friends?

There's a girl named Katie. She shared her story. She was 9 years old. She invited five girlfriends over. She hosted a **slumber** party. Slumber means sleep. A slumber party is a sleepover.

The girls went to the bathroom. They brought candles. They lit the candles. They turned off the light. They looked in the mirror. They **chanted**, "Bloody Mary." Chanting means to say something over and over again.

Katie said, "We saw an old woman with cuts on her face and chains around her neck and shoulders looking out of the mirror at us."

There are many stories on the Internet about people chanting "Bloody Mary."

CONSIDER THE EVIDENCE

Are ghosts real? Jadon and Lucy Billington are brother and sister. They're kids. They aren't afraid of ghosts. They talk to dead people. They live in England. Their house is haunted. They have over 10 ghost friends. One of these ghosts is their grandmother. Their mom said, "One night I was watching TV. And I said to Jadon, if they are really here now, ask one of them to tug at my trouser leg. Jadon asked. Then, a few seconds later, I felt something prod my leg. And I saw with my own eyes my trousers move. ... They also made the television go fuzzy when Jadon asked one to prove that he was there."

The shower curtain caught on fire. The girls screamed. They ran out of the bathroom.

An older boy heard their screams. He ran into the bathroom. He put out the fire. The girls got in trouble. Their parents thought the girls set the fire. Katie said the candles were 6 feet (2 meters) away. She said, "I know for a fact that we did not touch that shower curtain with a candle."

The girls believed in Bloody Mary. They thought they had **summoned** her ghost. Summon means to call forth.

Ghosts are spirits of dead people.

Most parents don't believe in "Bloody Mary."

There's another girl named Sara. She shared her story. She went to her friend's slumber party. There were three girls. They went into the bathroom at 3:00 a.m. They looked into the mirror. They chanted "Bloody Mary." They did this 13 times. They saw swirling smoke. They saw a scary old woman. Bloody Mary was looking at them.

They screamed. One girl turned the light on. Bloody Mary was gone. Her friend's mother didn't believe the girls. She made the girls go to bed. Sara said they stayed awake. She said, "We knew what we had seen."

Chapter Two

DARE TO SCARE

How is "Bloody Mary" a dare? What is the ritual for summoning Bloody Mary? What does Bloody Mary look like?

"Bloody Mary" is a **dare**. It's a fear test. It's a game. It's mostly played by kids. It's played at slumber parties. They tell stories about Bloody Mary. They dare each other. They summon Bloody Mary. They scare themselves.

There's a **ritual**. Rituals are formal events. They have certain steps. First, you must find a dark room. People usually use bathrooms. Bathrooms have large mirrors. Second, you light candles. Third, you chant "Bloody Mary." Do this several times. Most stories say to chant her name at least three times. Last, you wait. You see if Bloody Mary shows up in the mirror.

Some people light incense. The smoke protects you.

Some people say they see blood in the toilet water.

Bloody Mary appears as a **corpse**. Corpses are dead bodies. Bloody Mary is covered in blood. Some girls say they see a headless Bloody Mary. Some say they only see blood. Blood drips down the mirror.

Bloody Mary is mostly evil. Nobody knows how she'll react. She can scream. She can curse. She can choke. She can steal souls. She can drink blood. She can scratch out eyes. She can make people crazy. She can drag people into the mirror. Not knowing what will happen is part of the fun.

Some people think Bloody Mary tells the future.

Bloody Mary is female. She had a **violent** death. Violent means caused by physical force. Some stories say she died in a car accident. Some stories say she was killed. Some stories say she was a witch.

Bloody Mary wasn't always scary. Girls played this game a long time ago. They walked up stairs. They did this backward. They held a candle. They held a mirror. They did this in a dark house. They looked into the mirror. They wanted to see their future husband's face. But some girls saw a skull instead. This meant they wouldn't get married. The legend of Bloody Mary has changed.

REAL-WORLD
CONNECTION

There's a new "Bloody Mary" game. It's called the "Charlie Charlie Challenge." Teens summon devils. They film themselves. They share their videos. There's a special way to summon. They take a piece of paper. They draw a square. They separate the square into four sections. They write "Yes" in two sections. They write "No" in the other sections. They take two pencils. They lay them on top of the paper. They make a cross with the pencils. They say, "Charlie, Charlie, are you here?" They ask questions. They wait for the pencils to move. The pencils point to "Yes" or "No." Charlie haunts players who don't say good-bye before ending the game.

Chapter Three

THERE'S SOMETHING ABOUT MARY

Who is Mary? What are the different stories about Mary?

Many believe Bloody Mary is Mary Worth. Worth lived a long time ago. She was beautiful. She was **vain**. Vain means she admired herself. She looked in the mirror a lot. She had a bad accident. Her face was messed up. She became ugly. No one could look at her. She stayed away from mirrors. Seeing herself would make her crazy. One night, she looked in a mirror. She saw her ugly face. She screamed. She cried. She wanted her old face back. She walked into the mirror. She said she'd hurt anyone who found her.

To summon Mary Worth, people chant, "I believe in Mary Worth."

SPOTLIGHT BIOGRAPHY

Mary I was Queen of England and Ireland. She was born in 1516. Her father was King Henry VIII. Her mother was Catherine of Aragon. She ruled in the 1550s. She ruled for 5 years. She was known as "Bloody Mary." She brought the Catholic religion back to England. She killed people who disagreed with her. She killed Protestants. Protestants practiced a different religion. Queen Mary I burned over 300 people. She burned them at the stake. She jailed dozens of people. These people died in jail. Hundreds of people escaped to other countries. They wanted to get away from Bloody Mary. Mary thought she was saving people's souls.

There's another story about Mary Worth. Worth was a witch. She lived in Chicago. She lived during the Civil War. She caught runaway slaves. She kept them in her barn. She did dark magic on them. She hurt them. People found out what she was doing. They burned her alive. Her ashes were buried on her land. A hundred years later, a house was built on her land. Scary things happened. Worth haunted the house.

Some believe Mary Johnson is Bloody Mary. Johnson was a witch. She was burned at the stake.

To summon Mary Johnson, people chant, "Come, Mary Johnson, come."

There are many different "Mary" stories.

Some believe Mary Whales is Bloody Mary. Whales's mom died giving birth to her. Her dad hated Mary. He blamed her for his wife's death. He treated her badly. He dressed her in rags. He didn't feed her. Mary grew older. She looked more like her mom. Her dad couldn't stand it. He killed her. She haunted her dad. Her dad saw Mary in mirrors. He saw her glowing red eyes. He saw her bloody face. She reached out of the mirror. She clawed his face.

Some believe Mary Weatherby is Bloody Mary. Weatherby was stabbed to death. Her husband did it. She appears in mirrors. She chases people with a bloody knife.

Chapter Four

MAGIC AND MIRRORS

What do people believe about mirrors?
Why are mirrors important in magic?

Bloody Mary is a mirror witch. Mirror witches are in fairy tales. "Snow White" is a popular fairy tale. It has a magic mirror. It has a mirror witch. Stories about evil mirror witches appeared in the 1970s. These stories are about Bloody Mary. Chanting "Bloody Mary" is like casting spells. So, it's like magic.

Don't break a mirror. This could bring bad luck. Many people believe this to be true. They believe in magic. Mirrors have been used in magic. This has been happening since ancient times. People believed mirrors could tell the future. People just had to stare into mirrors.

Mirrors are called looking glasses.

People die. Families of the dead covered their mirrors. Or mirrors were turned to the wall. This was a way to respect the dead. It set ghosts free. It kept ghosts from getting trapped.

Some people thought mirrors were **portals**. Portals are doorways. They let ghosts travel through different worlds.

People thought looking in mirrors was bad. Being vain invites the devil. Many stories about Mary are about her being vain. This is why she's trapped in mirrors.

Mirrors were covered to avoid seeing the face of Death.

INVESTIGATION TIPS

- Talk to people who have played the "Bloody Mary" game. Ask them why they did it. Ask them how they felt. Ask them what happened.

- Count the mirrors in your house. Include anything that reflects images. Draw a map. Mark where all the mirrors are.

- Read the 45th Parallel Press book about ghost hunters. Learn what it means to be a ghost hunter. Learn how to find ghosts.

- Research different ways to summon Bloody Mary.

- Sit in a dark room. Sit 3 feet (1 meter) away from a mirror. Stare at your face. Do this for 10 minutes. Pay attention to how your face changes.

Chapter Five

SEEING THINGS

How do scientists explain Bloody Mary? How does Alan Dundes explain Bloody Mary?

Many people swear they have seen Bloody Mary. Scientists disagree. They don't think Bloody Mary is real.

People stare into a mirror. They do this in the dark. They do this for a long time. Scientists say this can cause **hallucinations**. People see things that aren't there. Their eyes play tricks on them. Their minds play tricks on them.

Scientists think people see their own faces. But their faces seem to melt. People's brains block out senses. They have a hard time recognizing things. They see strange images of themselves. This is called the Caputo Effect. (Giovanni Caputo is a scientist.)

Spinning messes up people's vision even more.

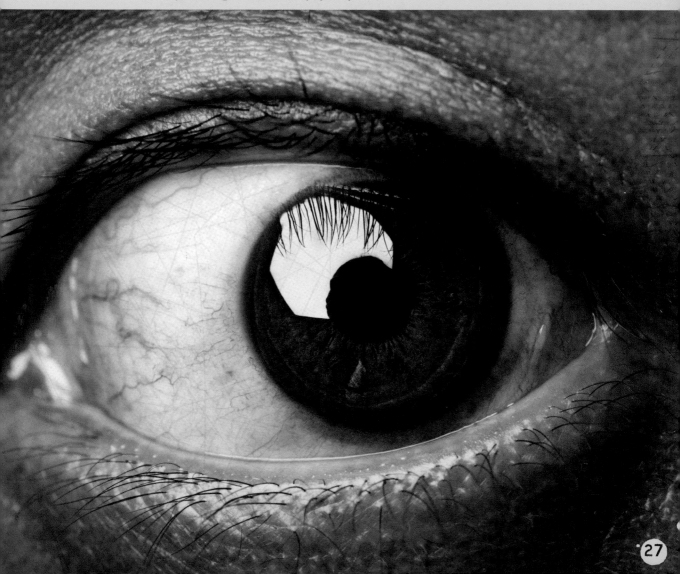

EXPLAINED BY SCIENCE

Light is made of traveling waves. It travels at high speeds. It hits an object. Light energy has to go somewhere. It passes through clear objects. It disappears into dark objects. It reflects back on shiny objects. These shiny objects are mirrors. Mirrors have smooth surfaces. This means they reflect light. Rough surfaces scatter light. When light hits, it hits at a certain angle. Mirrors catch the light. They throw it back out. They do this at the same angle. Light bounces and hits our eyes. Our eyes see a mirror image. Some people think mirrors switch right and left. This looks like a reversed image. But mirrors don't do this. They switch back and front.

Alan Dundes studied **folklore**. Folklore is about stories. It's about traditions. Dundes studied Bloody Mary. He said Bloody Mary is part of **coming-of-age** rituals. This is a stage between childhood and adulthood.

Playing "Bloody Mary" is exciting. But it's also scary. This is what growing up is like. Dundes thinks "Bloody Mary" helps teens. It lets them deal with scary life changes. It lets them deal with their fears and worries.

Real or not? It doesn't matter. Bloody Mary lives in people's imaginations.

Bloody Mary has inspired many movies and books.

DID YOU KNOW?

- Bloody Mary has many names. Other names are Bloody Bones and Black Agnes.

- *Svarte Madame* means "Black Madame." Madame means woman. It's the Swedish version of Bloody Mary. People go to a mirror. They say, "I don't believe in you, Svarte Madame." They say this 12 times. Then, the woman appears. She has black skin. She has green hair. She has red teeth. She has glowing yellow eyes.

- *Kuchisaka-onna* means "Slit-Mouth Woman." This version is from Japan. The woman was a warrior's wife. She cheated on her husband. The husband got mad. He slit her mouth from ear to ear. The woman was cursed. She can never die. She wanders the world. People see her scar. They feel bad for her. She asks if she's pretty. She kills people who say she's ugly.

- *La Llorona* is the Hispanic version. She cries a lot. She drowned her children. She searches for their souls. She calls for them.

- There's a story about a girl who didn't believe. She said, "I don't believe in Mary Worth." She left the bathroom. She tripped. She broke her hip.

- Some rituals include chanting at midnight. Some include spinning around. Some include rubbing one's eyes. Some include running the water.

- There's a saying. It was popular in 19th-century England. It states, "If you look in a mirror too long, you are sure to see the devil."

CONSIDER THIS!

Take a Position: Reread Chapter Three. There are many ideas about who Mary is. Which one do you think makes the most sense? Why do you think so? Argue your point with reasons and evidence.

Say What? Reread Chapter Two. Explain how to play the "Bloody Mary" game. Explain each step. Make sure you list the steps in order. Think of another dare game. Explain the steps to a friend.

Think About It! "Bloody Mary" is a dare game. Why do people do dares? Why do people like to be scared? Think about a time you did a dare. Why did you do it?

LEARN MORE

- Pulliam, June Michele, and Anthony J. Fonseca, eds. *Ghosts in Popular Culture and Legend*. Santa Barbara, CA: Greenwood, 2016.

- Young, Judy Dockrey, and Richard Young. *Favorite Scary Stories of American Children*. Little Rock, AR: August House, 2005.

GLOSSARY

chanted (CHANT-id) repeated over and over again

coming-of-age (KUHM-ing UHV AYJ) stage between childhood and adulthood

corpse (KORPS) dead body

dare (DAIR) a fear test, to challenge someone to do something scary

folklore (FOHK-lor) the study of stories and traditions

hallucinations (huh-loo-suh-NAY-shuhnz) experiences of seeing something that is not there

portals (POR-tuhlz) windows or doorways into other worlds

ritual (RICH-oo-uhl) formal event that has a series of actions or steps

slumber (SLUHM-bur) sleep

summoned (SUHM-uhnd) called forth

vain (VAYN) admiring oneself too much

violent (VYE-uh-luhnt) caused by physical force

INDEX

ABOUT THE AUTHOR

Dr. Virginia Loh-Hagan is an author, university professor, former classroom teacher, and curriculum designer. She tried playing "Bloody Mary." But she was too scared. She lives in San Diego with her very tall husband and very naughty dogs. To learn more about her, visit www.virginialoh.com.